Biomes
of the World

TUNDRA

ELIZABETH KAPLAN

BENCHMARK BOOKS

MARSHALL CAVENDISH
NEW YORK

Benchmark Books
Marshall Cavendish Corporation
99 White Plains Road
Tarrytown, New York 10591-9001

©Marshall Cavendish Corporation, 1996

Series created by Blackbirch Graphics, Inc.

For Julie, for her sense of humor—E. K.

Printed and bound in Hong Kong.

Library of Congress Cataloging-in-Publication Data

Kaplan, Elizabeth.
    Tundra / by Elizabeth Kaplan.
        p.   cm. — (Biomes of the world)
Includes bibliographical references and index.
ISBN 0-7614-0080-X (lib. bdg.) — ISBN 0-7614-0078-8 (set)
        1. Tundras—Juvenile literature. [1. Tundras. 2. Tundra ecology.
3. Ecology. 4. Arctic regions.] I. Title. II. Series.
GB572.K36   1995
551.4'53—dc20   95-2192
                                                                       CIP
                                                                        AC

Contents

Introduction

People traveling in an airplane often marvel at the patchwork patterns they see as they look down on the land. Fields, forests, grasslands, and deserts, each with its own identifiable color and texture, form a crazy quilt of varying designs. Ecologists—scientists who study the relationship between living things and their environment—have also observed the repeating patterns of life that appear across the surface of the earth. They have named these geographical areas biomes. A biome is defined by certain environmental conditions and by the plants and animals that have adapted to these conditions.

The map identifies the earth's biomes and shows their placement across the continents. Most of the biomes are on land. They include the tropical rainforest, temperate forest, grassland, tundra, taiga, chaparral, and desert. Each has a unique climate, including yearly patterns of temperature, rainfall, and sunlight, as well as certain kinds of soil. In addition to the land biomes, the oceans of the world make up a single biome, which is defined by its salt-water environment.

Looking at biomes helps us understand the interconnections between our planet and the living things that inhabit it. For example, the tilt of the earth on its axis and wind patterns both help to determine the climate of any particular biome.

The climate, in turn, has a great impact on the types of plants that can flourish, or even survive, in an area. That plant life influences the composition and stability of the soil. And the soil, in turn, influences which plants will thrive. These interconnections continue in every aspect of nature. While some animals eat plants, others use plants for shelter or concealment. And the types of plants that grow in a biome directly influence the species of animals that live there. Some of the animals help pollinate plants. Many of them enrich the soil with their waste.

Within each biome, the interplay of climatic conditions, plants, and animals defines a broad pattern of life. All of these interactions make the plants and animals of a biome interdependent and create a delicate natural balance. Recognizing these different relationships and how they shape the natural world enables us to appreciate the complexity of life on Earth and the beauty of the biomes of which we are a part.

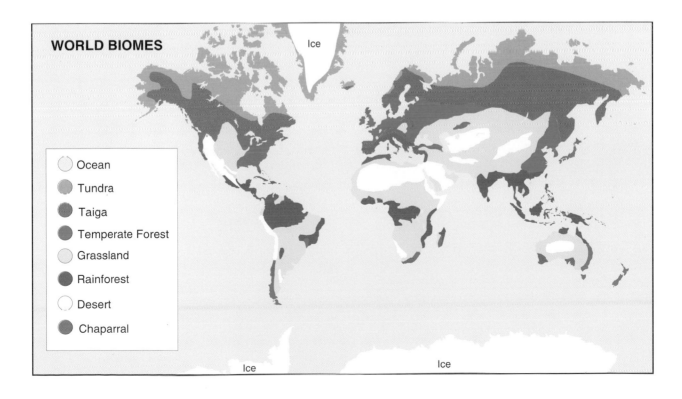

WORLD BIOMES

- Ocean
- Tundra
- Taiga
- Temperate Forest
- Grassland
- Rainforest
- Desert
- Chaparral

1

A Vast and Treeless Land

The tundra is a biome of sharp contrasts. In the winter, it is a cold, dark, windswept land where wildlife is rarely seen. In the summer, sunshine drenches the tundra. Herds of caribou hundreds of thousands strong spread out to graze, and waterbirds from all over the world converge on their summer nesting grounds. The land is frozen solid in the winter, but in summer it is soft and soggy, dotted with puddles and bogs. Although the tundra has the densest population of mosquitoes of any place on Earth, fewer people live on the tundra than in any other biome.

The tundra is the earth's coldest biome. The arctic tundra rings the northern part of the world, sweeping across Alaska, northern Canada, around the edges of Greenland, and across northern Scandinavia and northern regions of Russia,

Opposite:
The still beauty of the autumn tundra stretches beyond Scott Peak, Alaska, in the distance.

7

including Siberia. The alpine tundra is found in scattered patches on cold, windy mountaintops throughout the world. Trees cannot grow on the tundra because the soil remains frozen inches below the surface. This permanently frozen layer of soil is called permafrost. The lack of trees and the permafrost are the defining features of the tundra biome.

Beneath the Surface: Permafrost

Permafrost lies beneath more than 20 percent of the earth's surface. In some regions, the permafrost is patchy—the ground freezes in some spots and thaws in others. On the tundra, however, the permafrost never thaws. It forms a continuous underground layer in those regions where the climate is very cold and average annual temperatures rarely rise above -18° F (-8° C).

In the winter, the tundra freezes completely. When the air warms up in the late arctic spring, the surface of the ground above the permafrost begins to thaw. This thawing layer of soil and rock is called the active layer. In some areas, the active layer is less than 1 foot (30 centimeters) thick. In other places, the active layer extends down more than 3 feet (91 centimeters). Since the lower portions of the active layer do not thaw completely until the middle of the summer, most tundra plants have adapted to grow only in the top 4 to 10 inches (10 to 25 centimeters) of the active layer. The shallow depth of this thawed soil above the permafrost prevents trees from growing to their full height. Only smaller plants that send out roots in dense mats in the top part of the active layer are able to thrive on the tundra.

Although the size of plants that can grow here is limited by the permafrost, this frozen layer of soil is actually essential for plant growth in this biome. The tundra receives very little rain or snow. Most areas get about the same amount of precipitation as does the desert—1 to 10 inches (2 to 25 centimeters) per year. The permafrost traps this very scant precipitation by forming a barrier that prevents water from seeping deep into the ground. Moisture from rain and melting snow remains above the permafrost in the active layer, and plants absorb it through their roots. Without the permafrost to keep water in the active layer, tundra soil would be as dry as desert sand.

SLIP-SLIDING AWAY

Just as permafrost shapes the landscape of the arctic tundra, so does it have great influence on the tundra's community of alpine peaks. The permafrost that lies under the soil at high altitudes causes the soil on gently sloping mountainsides to slip away. This is called erosion, and it happens because the icy layer of permafrost acts like a slide. Wet soil on top of the permafrost simply flows down the slippery surface. The slipping soil can uproot any plants and trees in its path, furthering the process of erosion.

The movement of the soil, however, is often very slow and uneven. Terraces build up naturally where the slipping soil accumulates, and plants can easily take root. Such terraces help stabilize the mountainside, and give it a sculpted outline.

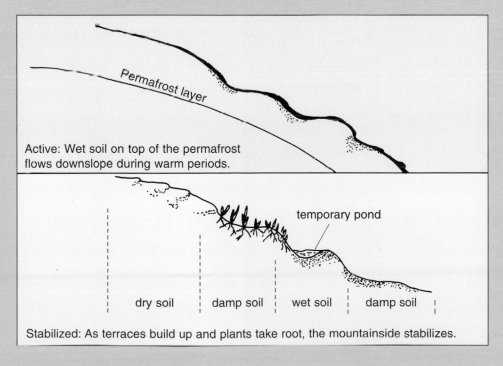

Permafrost layer

Active: Wet soil on top of the permafrost flows downslope during warm periods.

temporary pond

dry soil | damp soil | wet soil | damp soil

Stabilized: As terraces build up and plants take root, the mountainside stabilizes.

The Tundra Landscape

The permafrost not only affects the types of plants that grow on the tundra, it also shapes the tundra's landscape. Because of the permafrost barrier below the soil, water from melting ice and snow remains on the surface, forming lakes, marshes, bogs, and soggy ground. If you were to look out across an expanse of tundra on a bright summer day, you would see hundreds of large puddles and small ponds glistening in the sunshine. If you were to walk across the tundra, you would feel the softness of the earth as your feet sank down into the water-soaked moss.

During the fall, the freezing of water in the soil creates one of the tundra's more unusual features. As the ground freezes, it contracts. As it contracts, cracks are formed on the surface. The cracks create distinctive geometric patterns in the soil that look like polygons, flat shapes with at least three sides, which seem to fit into one another like the pieces of a giant jigsaw puzzle. In the

Water from the Mackenzie Delta flows throughout these polygons created by permafrost in the Northwest Territories, Canada.

spring and summer, water flows into the cracks between the polygon shapes. When the water freezes again in the fall, the cracks become even more evident, emphasizing the polygons. Where the soil is rocky, frost forces stones—both as small as pebbles and as large as boulders—up through the cracks. The stones give the shapes even more definition. Frost may even push the center of a polygon up, forming a mound a few inches to several feet high! This type of ground patterning is unique to the tundra.

An even more unusual feature of the tundra landscape occurs when large amounts of water freeze under its surface. Then a huge ice blister pushes up on the land, forming a circular or oval hill called a pingo. Pingos may rise sharply out of the flat plain of the tundra. They can take thousands of years to form, but they rarely reach heights of more than 300 feet (91 meters).

When a large pool of water freezes under the permafrost, it can push upward, resulting in a hill called a pingo. A pond has formed on the top of this pingo.

11

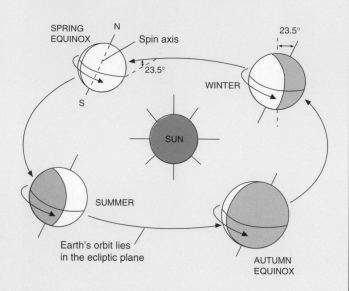

Seasons in the Northern Hemisphere

SPRING EQUINOX

N

Spin axis

23.5°

23.5°

S

WINTER

SUN

SUMMER

Earth's orbit lies
in the ecliptic plane

AUTUMN
EQUINOX

The 23.5° tilt of the earth's axis means that in summer,
not only is there more daylight, but the sun's rays
reach the earth's surface more directly through the
atmosphere and so lose less of their warmth. In winter,
not only is there less daylight, but the sun's rays have
to pass through more of the earth's atmosphere,
losing more of their warmth.

The Climate of the Tundra

The tundra is defined not only by its landscape but also by its climate. Winters are long, cold, and dark. The sun disappears below the horizon in the fall and does not rise again for months. This occurs because the Northern Hemisphere, where the arctic tundra is located, is tilted away from the sun in winter. This tilt of the earth prevents the sunlight from reaching the northernmost part of the planet. The lack of light and heat from the sun causes temperatures on the tundra to plunge to -94° F (-70° C). Winds shriek across the land, making the air even more frigid. For half of the year or longer, everything on the tundra is frozen solid.

The tundra slowly begins to thaw out in the spring, when the sun once again creeps above the horizon. By mid-summer, the sun makes an arc across the sky, soaring higher at noon and bowing low at night, never completely vanishing from the sky. During this season, the Northern Hemisphere of the earth is tilted toward the sun, so the northernmost part of the planet is always bathed in light. With this continuous sunshine, plants blossom quickly and animals remain active at all hours of the day and night. Summer temperatures sometimes rise as high as 85° F (30° C); but they do not stay high for long. Even in the middle of the summer, snow can fall on the tundra. The winds are still strong and will topple any plant that grows more than about 12 inches (30 centimeters) above the surface of the ground.

The length and severity of the tundra winter keep the permafrost from melting. Throughout the year, the wind prevents taller plants from growing. But the brief jubilation of summer, with its long hours of sunlight, gives the tundra a beautiful bloom of low-lying plant life that few places on Earth can match.

From the Tree Line to the North Pole

The arctic tundra, like the other biomes, includes a variety of plant life. You can see this diversity most clearly by starting at the tree line that separates the taiga (boreal, or evergreen, forest) from the tundra and traveling north. Just north of the tree line is the krummholz, a miniature forest of willows, birches, and gnarled evergreen trees that rarely reach heights of more than a few feet. Ground-hugging shrubs, grasses, and flowering plants grow in patches. Boggy areas sprout water-tolerant grasses. Where drainage is good, mosses thrive.

If you travel north from the regions dominated by bogs or krummholz, vegetation becomes sparse and the ground is littered with rocks and boulders. Lichens, which are algae and fungi that live together, grow in colorful crusty patches on the

Lichens are associations of fungi and algae, meaning that they live together as one organism.

13

THE MIDNIGHT SUN

It is summertime in the Arctic. You can sleep all day, stay up all night, and never have to turn on a light. In this land of the midnight sun, the middle of the night is as bright as a golden afternoon.

June 21, called the summer solstice, is the longest day of the year in the Northern Hemisphere. If you could spend the summer solstice in the Arctic Circle, you would see the sun shining through the night, dipping only briefly to touch the horizon at midnight. If you were to travel north on this day, you would note that the sun rose higher and higher in the sky, although it would still dip down toward the horizon in the middle of the night, as if to set. Imagine that you could travel all the way to the North Pole on the day of the solstice. You would see the sun make a complete circle high above the horizon. It would not set for months but would gradually sink lower and lower in the sky. Autumn would be a continuous twilight. Winter would be a three-month-long night.

The reason that days and nights are an entire season long at the North Pole is due to the tilt of the earth. The North Pole, which is the

northernmost point of our planet, is bathed in continuous sunlight all summer long. At the same time, the South Pole, the southernmost point of the earth, has perpetual night. As the earth orbits halfway around the sun, this tilt allows the sun's rays to reach the South Pole for months on end, while the North Pole receives no direct light for the entire three months of winter.

A view of the sun seen at midnight in an arctic village.

rocks. Clusters of tiny wildflowers grow in the soil between the rocks. The vegetation in this area is so sparse that some people refer to these rocky regions as the arctic desert. The arctic desert borders either the ice sheets, called glaciers, or the ice-packed Arctic Ocean. This is the limit of tundra plant life. However, tundra animals, such as polar bears and arctic foxes, often extend their range and venture far out onto the ice pack to hunt marine mammals that thrive in the cold, crystal waters of the world's northernmost ocean.

The History of the Tundra

The arctic tundra is the world's youngest biome. It was formed after the retreat of the last set of continental glaciers, about 10,000 years ago. As the glaciers advanced and retreated, they scraped away the soil underneath them, leaving bare rock. Before tundra plants could take root in the Arctic, a thin layer of soil had to develop on top of these rocks.

Soil forms on the arctic tundra as it does elsewhere. Lichens growing on bare rock give off chemicals that react with the rock. These chemical reactions cause part of the rock to break off in tiny flakes, which are made up of different minerals. The minerals from the flakes of rock then react with organic material from the lichens or with organic material from other living things. The resulting mixture of minerals and organic material forms soil.

Soil forms very slowly on the tundra because the cold weather slows the rate at which chemical reactions occur. In the thousands of years since the glaciers retreated, only a very thin layer of soil has formed in the southern parts of the Arctic. In the northernmost parts, the land remains mostly bare rock. It has taken thousands of years for plants to become established in the arctic tundra's thin soil. Compared with tropical rainforests, which have existed for hundreds of thousands of years, and with the oceans, which have thrived for millions of years, the tundra is a very young biome indeed.

Colorful flowers, such as this cluster of Scamman's spring beauty, are adapted to life on the tundra.

2

Spring and Summer on the Tundra

Spring does not come to the tundra with the sprouting of young, green buds or the blooming of tender wildflowers. In the middle of March, the arctic tundra is buried under a layer of snow. Temperatures often dip well below zero. Blizzards can rage, and the wind sometimes howls fiercely. What makes for spring in the tundra is the gradual increase of sunlight and the lengthening of the tundra day.

A Transition to Spring

The first day of winter in the Northern Hemisphere is December 21. This day, called the winter solstice, is the shortest day of the year in the Northern Hemisphere. Wherever you go on the arctic tundra on the day of the winter solstice,

Opposite:
A grizzly bear wanders through a summer field of lupine flowers on the tundra.

17

light levels will be low. But they will vary depending on your exact location. The southernmost reaches of the tundra get several hours of sunlight even on December 21. However, the northernmost regions of the arctic tundra remain in total darkness. From December 21 on, all parts of the tundra start to receive more and more light.

Although spring does not officially begin until the third week in March, a sense of spring comes to the arctic tundra when the sun first rises above the horizon. For most places on the arctic tundra, this happens sometime near the end of January or in early February. Daily average temperatures stay at well below zero. Snow depths may average almost 2 feet (60 centimeters). With the increased light, however, many of the tundra's year-round residents start to become more active in preparation for spring.

Spring is the Birthing Season

Spring is the birthing time for many winter residents of the tundra. Tundra wolves, sometimes called white wolves, wander the region's river valleys in packs of five to eight adults. The pack's two leaders, a male and a female, mate in the late winter or early spring. When it is time for the wolf pups to be born, the pregnant female finds a den. There she gives birth and raises her young, protected and in comfort. The pack stays around the den through the spring, bringing food to the growing pups.

Arctic foxes, like tundra wolves, also mate in the late winter or early spring, and look for dens in which to give birth and nurture their litters. While the fox cubs are young, the family stays together. The parents hunt for food to bring to the cubs. When the cubs can fend for themselves, later in the year, the family disbands, and each fox goes off on its own. Arctic hare and musk oxen are also active on top of the winter snow. As spring comes, arctic hare mate and prepare to raise their young. Like musk oxen, arctic hare feed on frozen plants.

Animals Rouse from Hibernation

Several animals wait out the winter by hibernating or by going into a state of rest. During hibernation, an animal has such a low body temperature and such a slow heartbeat that it is just barely alive. The ground squirrel is one tundra animal that hibernates through the winter. It comes out of hibernation when spring begins in the middle of March, and becomes fully active by the end of April.

Grizzly bears do not hibernate, but spend much of the winter in a state of deep sleep. Their heart rate and body temperature drop only slightly. They do not eat during the winter, and their bodies produce hardly any waste products. Female bears give birth to cubs, usually twins, during the winter. The cubs bury themselves in their mother's fur and stay snug, nursing until spring. Then the bears leave the den to roam the tundra.

For many kinds of mammals, spring is the season in which females give birth. These arctic fox pups wait by their den for their mother to return with food.

19

Migrants Return to the Tundra

In late winter and early spring, migrating birds and mammals return to the tundra. Among the first animals to arrive are the gyrfalcons, the world's largest falcon. They return to the Arctic in the middle of February to establish their territories and build their nests for April egg-laying.

In the early spring, herds of caribou migrate from the taiga to the tundra. The pregnant females leave first, usually in early March. They travel hundreds of miles to isolated calving grounds, where they give birth on the frozen tundra in late May.

Newborn caribou are spindly-legged and have sparse coats of fur. However, their diet of rich milk fattens them up quickly and helps spur their development. Within a few days, they can outrun their mothers. The caribou herds continue their migration to summer feeding grounds along the arctic coast. There, the males join up with the females and their young.

This dramatic aerial view shows a migrating herd of caribou that numbers at least 10,000.

Caribou herds vary in size from a few thousand on Canada's far northern arctic islands to more than half a million on the mainland of Canada. Large though this sounds, the North American caribou herds have been greatly reduced over the past hundred years. Today, there are probably fewer than 2 million caribou in all of North America. In 1900, however, more than 25 million caribou crossed the northern reaches of the continent. One herd would have contained as many as several million animals and taken a week or more to pass a single spot on its migration route.

In color, if not in numbers, the spring bird migration far surpasses that of the caribou. More than one hundred different kinds of birds make their way north to the tundra from the end of March until the beginning of June. At Point Barrow on the Alaskan arctic tundra, close to 1 million birds have been counted in just four weeks. Most of the birds that migrate to the tundra are waterfowl, such as ducks, geese, swans, gulls, and cranes and other wading birds. As the snow and ice melt in late May and early June, these birds thrive on the lake-dotted coastal plains. Certain birds of prey, including eagles and falcons, also migrate to the arctic tundra in the spring.

As spring sweeps the tundra, a very lonely, silent, snow-covered world is transformed into a plain of rich color, ringing with sound and teeming with life.

Bald eagles migrate to the tundra in the spring. Here, a majestic eagle expertly preys on a salmon.

THE MIGRATION OF THE POLAR BEAR

Most animals that migrate to the arctic tundra come from regions to the south. One animal, however, makes a summer migration to the tundra from the north. This is the polar bear, the Arctic's white giant that pads across the snow and ice on furred feet. Polar bears are actually as much at home in the ocean as they are on land. Males and non-pregnant females spend the winter traveling

Arctic foxes trail after a lone polar bear in hopes of eating the bear's left-over food.

across the ice packed against the arctic coast. They feast on seals that come up for air at breathing holes in the ice. Unless the polar bear is starving, it eats only the outer layers of fat—or blubber—on the seal's body. The rest is often eaten by arctic foxes, which frequently follow the polar bears far out onto the ice. Ravens and gulls may also peck away at the polar bear's leavings.

Polar bears are great wanderers; in fact, that is the name the Inuit people of Greenland have given the animals. Polar bears have been spotted swimming out in the open ocean 1,000 miles (1,609 kilometers) from the nearest shore. Some polar bears make their way north almost all the way to the North Pole. Others travel as far south as Iceland or even the St. Lawrence River in Quebec, Canada.

When the ice that covers the northern arctic waters begins to melt in the late spring and early summer, the polar bears usually return to the tundra. They scour the land for berries and birds' eggs, ducks and molting geese, and a variety of other animals. Even with ample food available, the summer is a difficult time of year for the polar bear. This animal, with its thick fur coat and an equally thick layer of insulating fat, is well adapted for the winter. But even the cool temperatures of the tundra in summer prove too warm for the polar bear. Some of them dig pits all the way down to the permafrost. There they stay for much of the summer, cooling their backs against the frozen ground.

Tundra Plants Come Back to Life

The blanket of snow that covers much of the tundra in the winter helps insulate plants from the cold and protects them from damaging winds. However, the snow cover keeps light from getting to the plants, which prevents photosynthesis (the process by which plants use the energy from sunlight to make food). So until enough snow melts to expose the leaves of the tundra plants to sunlight, these plants remain dormant.

Once the snow begins to melt, usually in May, tundra plants immediately begin making food for both growth and reproduction. Unlike plants that grow in warmer regions, most tundra plants can start photosynthesizing at temperatures just above freezing ($32°$ F [$0°$ C]).

Many tundra plants are evergreens. As their name implies, these plants remain green year-round and do not have to produce a new set of leaves in spring before they can photosynthesize. Even tundra plants that are not evergreens have some parts that stay green through the winter. For example, the bottom of the stalks of grasses remains green.

Tundra plants have a dense mat of roots that grows just under the surface of the ground. These roots immediately take up moisture from the melting snow. Collecting moisture is very important for tundra plants, because the high winds that blow across the land throughout the year can dry them out very quickly.

Growing low to the ground also helps to protect tundra plants from damage from strong winds. Low growth helps the tundra plants in another way as well. Because the earth gives off heat, the air tends to be warmer closer to the ground than it is a few feet above the ground. Plants that are warmer tend to grow faster, which is an advantage on the tundra because of the short growing season. Some tundra plants also grow in tight clumps, with a rosette pattern of leaves or with a rounded, pincushionlike base from which leaves and flowers poke out. With these arrangements, tundra plants trap heat, keeping

Within this small area of tundra ground cover there are several different species of plants that have rosette patterns, as well as dark colors that absorb sunlight for warmth.

temperatures close to the plant as much as twenty degrees warmer than the surrounding air. Also, older leaves on the outside of the plant die, but stay in place to shelter the younger leaves toward the center.

Tundra plants also create their own warmth. Many have dark leaves and stems. Dark colors absorb sunlight and radiate it as heat. A dense mat of hair covers the leaves of many of these plants, trapping heat close to the leaves, while at the same time letting light through to the leaves' surface. The function of the layers of hair is similar to that of the glass panes in a greenhouse, which allow sunlight to enter, but prevent heat from escaping.

By the third week in June, most snow patches have melted on the tundra. The migrants have returned. Many of the birds have built nests and laid their eggs. Most of the animals have given birth to their young. Plants are in bloom. Summer is in full swing on the tundra.

Plants Adapt for the Summer

June 21 is the summer solstice, the longest day of the year. On the northernmost parts of the tundra, the sun shines all day and all night. On the southernmost part of the tundra, the sun may dip below the horizon for several hours, but the sky never becomes completely dark. Although the sun shines for many hours of the day in the arctic summer, the light comes in at a low angle and is less intense than in other biomes.

Summer temperatures on the tundra average around 50° F (10° C). In some parts of the tundra, however, record highs of 85° F (29° C) are reached. Temperatures also often drop below freezing, and summer snows are not unusual.

Whatever day-to-day conditions are in a particular place on the tundra in summer, this general rule remains true: Summer is a time for growth, for reproduction in plants, and for preparing for winter.

The main problem facing tundra plants is how to grow and reproduce in the few short months of summer. Many store food in their roots or in underground stems. They convert this food into energy as soon as the snow melts. They use the energy to bud and flower quickly. Many arctic flowers have a deep-dish shape, much like a satellite dish. The flowers rotate, tracking the sun as it moves across the sky. By moving to follow the sun, the flower collects the maximum amount of sunlight it can in a day. The dish shape helps focus sunlight on the center of the flower, where seed production takes place. The light warms the plant, allowing it to grow faster and the seeds to develop more quickly.

Even with these adaptations for collecting the maximum amount of sunlight and warming up the center of the flower, for some tundra plants, the growing season is just too short to allow the plant to complete seed production. Such plants produce seeds in stages over several years. One year, the flower buds and blooms. The next year, the fruit forms. The third year, the seeds in the fruit ripen and finally are dispersed.

Most tundra plants produce seeds that are scattered by the wind. Because the winds are strong throughout the year, tundra seeds are dispersed in all seasons. The rapid scattering of these seeds has caused many tundra plants to proliferate throughout the Arctic. Wind-borne seeds are commonly carried over the North Pole and across the narrow seas that separate Asia from North America and North America from Greenland.

Before seeds can form, however, flowers have to be fertilized. Some flowers are fertilized when bees, flies, and other traveling insects rub them with pollen from another plant. Other flowers are self-fertilized: They receive pollen from their own plants. Many tundra plants can also make new plants without producing seeds. These plants send out underground stems, which are called called runners. New plants can then shoot up from the runners.

A bumblebee fertilizes a tundra flower with pollen.

Spring and Summer on the Tundra

Summer Changes in Tundra Animals

As the snow melts, year-round tundra residents change to adjust to the new season. Among the most obvious changes are changes in color. Ptarmigan, arctic foxes, and arctic hare are pure white in the winter. With their white fur or feathers, they blend in perfectly with the snow, camouflaging themselves from their predators or their prey. When the snow begins to melt in the late spring or early summer, these animals begin to change color again. They become a mottled brown or gray color, which blends in with the ground. This kind of camouflage is especially important, because the lack of trees and bushes of any height on the tundra means that there are very few places where animals can hide from their predators.

The musk ox is one of the few tundra animals that does not change coat color from winter to summer. Musk oxen eat plants, so they do not need to conceal themselves from their prey. They also do not need to hide from predators, because they are so big and sturdy and can form such tight herds that predators rarely go after them. But musk oxen do shed their woolly, warm undercoat when the weather warms up in the summer. This fur floats across the tundra in tufts that birds then collect for lining their nests. Musk oxen fur is soft, light-weight, and very, very warm. People spin this fur into yarn to make hats and scarves that are prized throughout the northern regions.

Life in and on the Water

When the ice covering the lakes and rivers of the tundra melts, life abounds in and around these bodies of water. The arctic char, a fish closely related to the salmon, swim from the seas north of the tundra up the rivers that run through the tundra to fresh-water lakes, where they spawn. Grayling, also related to the salmon, are numerous in the fresh-water lakes of the arctic tundra. Eagles, peregrine falcons, grizzly bears, and polar bears often feed on these fish in the summertime.

27

Insect eggs and larvae (young insects that have not metamorphosed, or changed, into their adult form), lay buried along the banks of the tundra's lakes and rivers, or frozen in the ice. When summer weather arrives, these eggs and larvae thaw out. Even when temperatures warm to only a degree or two above freezing, tundra insect eggs can hatch and larvae can begin to feed and grow. The tundra's bogs, ponds, and lakes support huge numbers of mosquitoes, midges, caddisflies, dragonflies, and blackflies, all of which require water for part of their life cycles. Beetles, bumblebees, butterflies, moths, and many types of flies are also found on the tundra. In some places, insect life is so dense that there may be more than a million insects swarming in 1 square yard (0.8 square meter) of land. The plentiful insect life provides food for many types of migrant birds, but they are biting pests for many other animals.

A brown bear deftly catches a sockeye salmon from Brooks Falls in the Katmai National Park in Alaska.

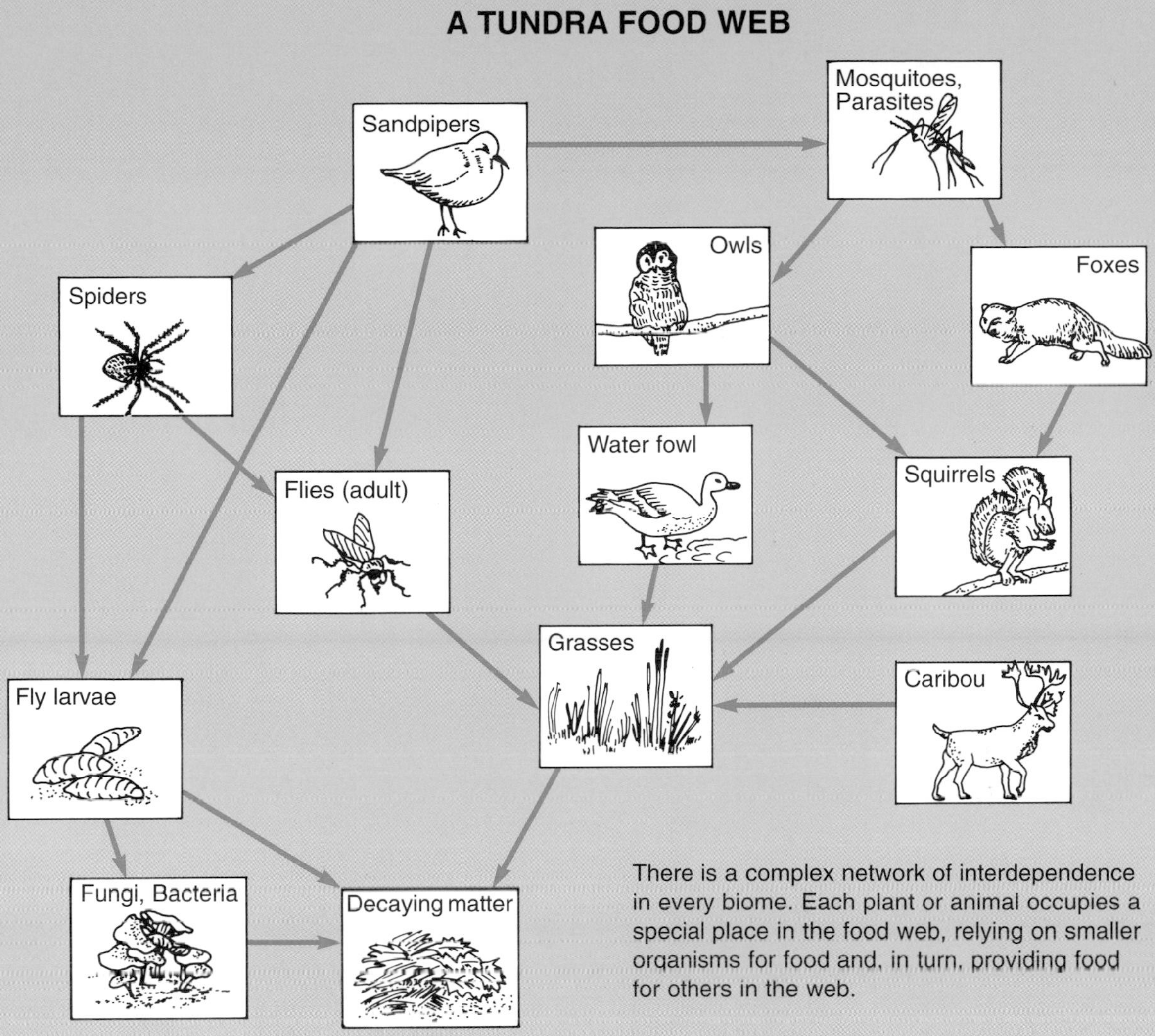

A TUNDRA FOOD WEB

Sandpipers

Mosquitoes, Parasites

Spiders

Owls

Foxes

Flies (adult)

Water fowl

Squirrels

Fly larvae

Grasses

Caribou

Fungi, Bacteria

Decaying matter

There is a complex network of interdependence in every biome. Each plant or animal occupies a special place in the food web, relying on smaller organisms for food and, in turn, providing food for others in the web.

The Summer Food Web

A food web is a diagram that shows the complex feeding relationships between all of the different animals that live in a community or biome. The arrows show how energy moves through the community. They point from the organism that does the eating to the one that is eaten. For example, in this summer food web of the tundra, an arrow points from the caribou to different tundra plants. The arrow indicates that the caribou eat the plants. What do some of the other tundra animals eat? Because of all the plants that thrive on the tundra in the summer, and all the animals that either migrate to the tundra or live there year-round, for a few short months, the tundra is transformed into one of the liveliest biomes on earth.

3

Fall and Winter on the Tundra

A grizzly bear and her cubs prance across the tundra, stopping from time to time to feast on crowberries, bearberries, and bilberries, which turn their teeth dark blue. Ground squirrels chatter to one another, gathering seeds for their underground storage bins deep in their burrows. Plants soak up the sunshine and use the energy to make food, which they will store in underground bulbs, roots, or stems. It's August on the tundra, and the sun is bright and warm. Nonetheless, animals and plants alike are preparing for the winter.

By September 21, when fall officially begins, the tundra may already have received its first dusting of snow. The hours of daylight have been steadily decreasing, and the sun, when it shines, is usually low in the sky. Temperatures are at or below the freezing point. The fall chill is settling over the land.

Opposite: Musk oxen have a thick underlining of fur that helps trap their body heat for warmth.

31

Animals That Leave the Tundra

Many of the animals that spend summer on the tundra do not stay for the winter season. By the end of the summer, many of the migrant birds have already headed south for the winter. The arctic tern makes its record migration each year from the arctic tundra all the way to the other end of the world—Antarctica. The 11,000-mile (18,000-kilometer) journey takes several months. These terns are usually long gone by early September. Other birds remain on the tundra a few weeks longer. Many different types of geese, for example, spend a month of intensive feeding along the coastal plains of the arctic tundra. The birds build up fat reserves, which they then use for energy during their long flight south. However, by the time the snowstorms start in earnest, usually by the middle of September, these geese, too, have left the tundra.

Caribou also leave the tundra soon after the snows start to fall. They often begin their migration in scattered bunches, joining as they converge on well-worn trails that the caribou have used for hundreds of years. These animals, like many of the migrant birds, are well filled out after their summer of feeding on arctic plants. They do not have as far to travel as most of the migrating birds do. They head, instead, for the evergreen forests of the taiga, several hundred miles south, where they are able to find more abundant food as well as shelter from the wind and snow.

Animals That Stay on the Tundra

The animals that stay on the tundra adopt one of two strategies for surviving the winter. Either they enter a period of hibernation or winter rest, or they remain active, searching for food throughout the season.

The ground squirrel is the tundra's only true hibernator. In early October, when the ground has frozen, the ground squirrel enters its burrow, curls up in a grass-lined nest, and settles into a state of sleep so deep that a casual observer might think the squirrel was dead. During hibernation, the ground squirrel's body temperature drops to just above freezing. Its heart rate slows from 200 beats per minute to only 5 beats per minute. Its breathing rate slows dramatically as well. Drawing on its reserves of fat, the ground squirrel hibernates through most of the fall, through the entire winter, and well into the spring.

Grizzly bears and pregnant polar bears enter dens in the middle or late fall and spend the winter in a sleep that is deep, but from which they can be roused. Grizzly bears usually find dens among rock formations, in holes or tunnels in hills, or in pits in the ground. Polar bears, on the other hand, often dig their dens in snowbanks. After the bears settle into their dens and fall asleep, their body temperatures drop slightly and their heart and breathing rates fall. In fact, female bears give birth to their cubs in the winter in their dens, without entirely rousing from their sleep during the birth process.

Small mammals, including lemmings, shrews, and voles, spend the winter in tunnels under the ground and beneath the snow. These animals, however, remain active throughout the winter. The lemming has a high body temperature but a short-haired coat, which does not hold in heat very well. The tundra's subzero temperatures and blasting winds would cause lemmings to freeze to death if they lived on the open tundra. Lemmings and other small mammals can survive the winter only because they live beneath the snow. Females make large nests with thick linings of leaves and grasses for insulation. There they will raise several litters of young throughout the winter.

Three types of birds stay on the tundra throughout the year: ptarmigan, ravens, and snowy owls. Ptarmigan are flocking birds related to chickens. Like chickens, ptarmigan rely on plants as their food. They eat buds and twigs that poke through the snow during the winter and spring months. They sleep in burrows in the snow. Ravens are birds common in temperate regions, as well as on the arctic tundra. They can survive the northern winter because they will eat anything— buds and berries, carrion (the meat of dead animals), food scraps and other garbage left by people, and small mammals. Snowy owls prey primarily upon small mammals. They live closer to the North Pole than does any other bird species. The snowy owl's favorite food is the lemming. To survive, it must eat as many as 1,600 lemmings each year.

The most obvious changes are seen in those arctic animals that spend fall and winter on top of the snow. Arctic hare, arctic foxes, and ptarmigan change color. Over the course of a few

A snowy owl holds a lemming in its mouth as it prepares to feed its chicks.

Arctic hares, as well as other arctic animals, change color as the seasons change. In spring and summer, an arctic hare is brown (below). In autumn, a hare will begin to turn white for winter (above).

weeks, these animals go from a mottled brown or gray, to include patches of white, to pure white. These color changes allow them to blend in more easily with a background of snow. They also grow thicker, warmer coats for the winter. The mammals, including musk oxen, foxes, and hare, develop a thick underlining of fur that helps trap body heat close to the body. On the tops and bottoms of their feet, foxes and hare grow fur, and ptarmigan grow feathers. These coverings act like slippers that keep the animals warm as they walk over the snow.

THE NORTHERN LIGHTS

There is no sun to brighten the winter sky of the arctic tundra. But this region boasts a unique light show that is not often seen in most other parts of the world: the northern lights. Also called the aurora borealis, the northern lights appear as a rippling curtain of multicolored lights hanging in the dark sky. Blues and greens are the most common colors, but reds, oranges, and yellows also appear. Although the aurora borealis usually looks like vertical streaks, the dancing lights may also form flashing arcs or shimmering fans. You can see the northern lights on many clear winter nights on the arctic tundra.

Myths surrounding the northern lights are common. The Vikings believed that the lights were flames of the fire god's ovens. People from the northern Germanic tribes of Europe considered the lights to be reflec-

tions off the metal shields of the Valkyrie, mythical warrior women. North American Indians who live near the tundra considered the northern lights to be the spirits of unborn children playing in the sky.

The scientific explanation for the northern lights is as dramatic as some of the myths are. Electrical storms occur on the surface of the sun. During these storms, the sun shoots out streams of tiny, energy-charged particles called electrons. These streams of electrons, which concentrate near the poles, pass by the earth. When one of these electrons collides with another particle in the earth's atmosphere, a tiny flash of light is given off. The northern lights result when billions of these collisions occur, lighting up the sky in beautiful patterns.

Billions of colliding electrons in the earth's atmosphere result in a spectacular phenomenon called the aurora borealis.

Winter on the Tundra

By the time winter officially begins, on December 21, the tundra has been frozen for several months. Although the days have been getting shorter and shorter for months, the first day of winter is the shortest day of the year. This day is called the winter solstice. Because the northern part of the earth is tilted away from the sun in winter, the northernmost part of the tundra is in complete darkness during the late fall and early winter. The southernmost regions of the tundra may have a few hours of sunlight each day during this part of the year, but most of the time it is as dark as night.

About 1 to 3 feet (0.3 to 0.9 meter) of snow falls during the winter on most parts of the tundra. As the wind sweeps across the tundra, it blows the land bare of snow in some places and causes deep drifts in others. Average temperatures are quite low, around -20° F (-29° C). Because of the strong winds, however, the air often feels twenty degrees colder. In such weather, the danger of frostbite is very great. Exposed skin can freeze in only a minute.

Plants Adapt to the Winter

The arctic tundra is a harsh place in winter for plants and animals alike. Yet some organisms survive quite well. For example, lichens simply freeze in the fall and winter. In the spring, they thaw out and continue growing. Seeds of many arctic plants will live through a freeze and grow and bloom when they thaw out. Scientists have found seeds of arctic plants that were frozen for 10,000 years. When the seeds were thawed out and planted, they bloomed as if they had never been frozen.

Tundra plants, however, do not always freeze solid in the winter. Plants underneath a blanket of snow are protected from the subzero temperatures. The snow insulates the plants, and holds temperatures at ground level right around freezing. In addition, many tundra plants have sap that acts as an antifreeze.

37

This sap contains chemicals that prevent the plant from freezing, even when temperatures drop far below freezing. This prevents ice crystals from forming in the plant's tissues and damaging them.

Winter Wildlife

If you were to travel to the tundra in winter, you would see very few animals. In a town on the tundra, you might be greeted by ravens perched on roofs or electric wires, waiting to pick out scraps from the garbage. On an isolated, windswept ridge, you might catch a glimpse of musk oxen munching on the exposed lichens. If you had both good eyesight and were patient, you might observe a flock of ptarmigan rise like a flurry of white snow from a snowbank and scatter to feed on exposed willow shoots. You could watch for an arctic hare pawing through a snowdrift to munch on a few dry tufts of grass. And if you were to fly low over the ice-packed seas north of the tundra, you might spot a polar bear that had just caught and killed a seal for dinner. An arctic fox might be standing nearby until the polar bear finished its meal, waiting to trot over and gnaw on the remains.

If you could somehow see beneath the snow, however, you would discover a whole different world than the relatively quiet one described above. Lemmings, shrews, and voles would be running through a network of tunnels in the snow and under the ground. They would be digging their way to buried plants and lichens, feeding on them throughout the winter. Weasels would be chasing after these small mammals, trapping them in their tunnels. Snowy owls would be scanning the frozen ground for any animal unwary enough to poke its whiskers above the snow cover.

In the winter, the web of life is simple on the tundra. The food chains are very short. Only the hardiest plants and animals can survive winter on the tundra—one of the longest, darkest, coldest winters on Earth.

HOW DO HUMANS SURVIVE THE TUNDRA WINTER?

Several different groups of people have traditionally made their homes on the arctic tundra. The tundra-dwellers of North America and Greenland are commonly known as Eskimos, which means "eaters of raw meat." However, this name is inaccurate, and some find it insulting. The North American tundra-dwellers prefer the names they call themselves: The eastern Canadians call themselves the Inuit; some of the western Canadians prefer Inuvialuit; the Alaskans go by the name Inupiat; and Greenlanders have still other names for their groups. All of these people share a common culture, including many ingenious ways of adapting to the cold winter of the tundra.

Tundra-dwellers have traditionally worn clothing made of caribou skin, because they have found it to be the lightest, yet warmest, material from which to make clothing. Throughout most of the year, they wore two pairs of pants. The inner pair was worn with the hair facing in, for warmth. The outer pair was worn with the hair facing out, for waterproofing. Tundra-dwellers also wore loose-hooded, big jackets called parkas. The hoods were lined with wolverine hairs, which are sharply pointed. When moisture from the wearer's breath formed on this fur, the pointed hairs would allow the water to drip right off.

Boots were often made from sealskin, which is highly waterproof, and were lined with bird's skin for warmth. The soles were made from different materials, depending on where the boots were to be worn. Boots used for walking on rough terrain were soled with walrus hide, which is exceptionally tough and durable. Boots used for winter hunting on snow and ice were soled with polar-bear hide, because the wearer could then sneak up on prey without making any sound.

A native boy from the village of Kaktovik, Alaska, wears a traditional jacket with a hair-lined hood to keep him warm and dry.

4

The Alpine Tundra

Imagine that you could walk up a mountain from its base to its rocky peak. At the bottom of the mountain, you would hike through a shady forest of broad-leaf trees. As you climbed higher up the mountain, you would enter an evergreen forest. The dense piles of pine needles would cushion your steps and give the forest a serene, quiet beauty. Climbing higher, you would come out of the forest onto a treeless, open environment studded with low plants. This is the alpine tundra. As you hiked farther up the mountain, the plants would thin out, and the rocks would become more and more prominent. You would trek among big boulders near the bottom of this rocky area. Higher up, the side of the mountain might be covered with gravel. Near the top of the mountain, the windswept rock would be free of soil and snow. Blasted by constant winds and deprived of moisture, the rocks at the very tip of the mountain would be devoid of life.

Opposite:
The alpine tundra has a beauty all its own. Here, velvety elk bulls stand atop a Colorado mountain, with a view of the evergreen forest below.

Comparing the Alpine and Arctic Tundra

Like the arctic tundra, the alpine tundra is a treeless biome that is dominated by a variety of low-lying plants. The plants of the alpine tundra, like those of the arctic tundra, are adapted to short, cool summers, and high winds year-round. Because of these similar growing conditions, many species of arctic tundra plants also thrive on the alpine tundra.

The alpine tundra, however, presents some unique challenges to the organisms that inhabit it. The alpine tundra, unlike the arctic tundra, gets significant amounts of sunlight throughout the year. This light is much more intense than the light that hits the arctic tundra. The light that shines on the arctic tundra passes through a thick layer of the earth's atmosphere. This helps filter out certain high-energy light waves, such as ultraviolet light, which can damage plants and other

VISITING THE ALPINE TUNDRA

Because the alpine tundra is found only at the tops of very high mountains, you might think that it would be difficult to visit these wild, open places. It is true that most patches of alpine tundra cannot be reached easily. It requires at least a few hours, if not a few days, of hiking up rugged trails from base camps in the forests or valleys below. However, there are places in the alpine tundra that are accessible by paved roads.

One of those places is Pikes Peak, in Colorado. A well-traveled road goes directly to the top of this 14,110-foot (4,304-meter) mountain. Another is Rocky Mountain National Park, near Estes Park, Colorado. Reaching most of the tundra regions in this popular park does not demand a hike. Instead, you can drive to the tundra on Trail Ridge Road, which winds through the park. If you are in the state of Washington, you can take the road to Obstruction Point, in Olympic National Park, and step out of your car onto the alpine tundra. If you are in New England, you can reach alpine tundra by driving the road that leads to the summit of Mount Washington, in the White Mountain National Forest in New Hampshire.

Although the alpine tundra is accessible, visitors should be aware of the fragility of its ecosystem. One step off the path can destroy an entire community of miniature alpine plants. Because of the short growing season, it takes years for any disturbed area of the tundra to recover.

living things. The higher you go in elevation, however, the thinner the atmosphere becomes. At the upper regions of most mountains, the atmosphere is very thin. The thin atmosphere lets more ultraviolet light through. Inhabitants of the alpine tundra have developed ways of protecting themselves from high levels of ultraviolent light.

The alpine tundra generally gets more rainfall than the arctic tundra. Because of the slope of the mountain, however, moisture does not necessarily remain where it falls. It may run off a mountain very rapidly. In many places on the alpine tundra, water does not collect in the top layer of the soil, as it does in the arctic tundra. The soil is dry and dusty, and blows away easily in the mountain winds.

The slope of a mountain also causes rock and soil to slip downward. Significant movement can take centuries, or it can occur suddenly in a violent rock or mud slide. Snow, too, can thunder down the mountainside in an avalanche. This movement can damage or destroy life on the alpine tundra.

How Plants Adapt to the Alpine Tundra

Plants that live on the alpine tundra have developed many of the same adaptations as arctic tundra plants. They grow low to the ground in response to stress caused by the winds. They grow in pin-cushion or rosette forms, trapping blowing soil and holding heat near the plants. Many have dark-colored, hairy leaves, which help the plants absorb and hold heat. These adaptations make it easier for plants to carry out life functions in the cool alpine environment.

Many alpine plants also store food in underground roots or stems. They get a head start on growth, using the stored energy in this food. Most alpine plants can start to make more food through the process of photosynthesis, at temperatures just above freezing. These plants can start growing even during the cool alpine spring, and may extend their growing season into the frosty mountain autumn.

THE MARVELOUS MOUNTAIN GOAT

The rocky peaks and steep cliff faces of mountains are an unlikely home for any type of large animal. Mountain goats, however, do thrive in these slippery, wind-lashed places, jumping from rock to ledge, seemingly unconcerned about the height or any danger. Mountain goats have found a sparse but sure food supply among these rocky outcrops. Tufts of grass sprout in a teaspoonful of soil sheltered in the crack of a stone; moss springs up under a dripping overhang; lichens grow in crusty patches on otherwise bare rock. Only a few surefooted animals like the mountain goat can safely reach such isolated plants.

These animals are superbly adapted to life in the high mountains. They have thick, shaggy coats that keep them warm when the wind and snow blow. Their legs are very muscular, which enables them to make long leaps from one high ledge to another. Their tendons are springy, absorbing the shock of those bracing bounds. Their hooves have strong, gripping toes and a suction-cuplike pad, making the animals secure on even the most slippery rock. Because of these features, mountain goats make climbing the world's most rugged mountains look easy.

Different kinds of mountain goats thrive in the high ranges throughout the world. The Rocky Mountain goat and bighorn sheep are found on rocky peaks throughout the western United States and Canada. Alpine ibex grace the slopes of the Alps. Chamois can be found in high pockets in the mountains of western Asia. The Himalayas and the Tibetan plateau have argali and markhor, large long-horned sheep and goats. All of these animals survive where other large mammals—including their predators—dare not go.

Mountain goats are perfectly adapted to their environment and can leap from ledge to ledge with ease.

Many alpine plants, like many arctic plants, flower and set seed very quickly. This adaptation allows them to reproduce successfully during the short alpine summer. Other alpine plants produce buds, fruits, and seeds that can withstand freezing. Like similar plants in the Arctic, they take several years to produce one set of seeds—another adaptation to a short, cool growing season. Finally, many alpine plants can reproduce by sending out runners on or under the ground. Like arctic plants, these plants can colonize an area quickly without having to take the time to produce seeds.

Some alpine plants resemble arctic plants in that they send out a shallow mat of roots. This adaptation allows them to soak up surface moisture quickly before it runs off the mountain. Other alpine plants, however, have deep taproots. These thick, sturdy roots help anchor plants in soil that is slowly slipping down the mountain. Taproots even help prevent the soil from eroding by holding it firmly in place.

How Do Animals Adapt to the Alpine Tundra?

Alpine animals, like arctic animals, share many adaptations to the harsh tundra environment. Some, including elk, moose, foxes, hare, and songbirds, come to the alpine tundra during the summer season, but migrate to warmer regions down the mountain during the fall. Others, notably the marmot, hibernate in underground dens to escape the winter cold.

Those animals that remain active on the alpine tundra during the winter use a combination of strategies to survive. Most rely on thick fur or feathers as insulation from the cold. Mountain goats and bull elk, for example, have thick winter coats that help them stay warm.

Smaller mammals that stay active throughout the alpine winter seek shelter from the cold. Pikas, small chipmunklike animals related to rabbits, spend most of the time in their dens among the rocks and boulders. They emerge to collect grass clippings that they have cut during the summer and stored

A Rocky Mountain pika briskly clips grass to store under rocks for the winter.

under rocks for their winter food supply. Pocket gophers are burrowing animals that spend winter and summer underground. The soil and snow cover insulate pocket gophers from the cold. Like pikas, pocket gophers also store food for the winter, in underground storage chambers off their network of tunnels.

Ptarmigan are the only birds that stay on the alpine tundra in the winter. These are the same chickenlike birds that live on the arctic tundra. Ptarmigan have feathered feet that protect them from the cold. They are pure white in the winter, blending in with the snow, and are a mottled gray and brown in the summer, blending in with the rocky ground.

Plants and Animals Unique to the Alpine Tundra

Alpine-tundra regions around the world share many of the same types of plants and animals. For example, alpine sorrel, a plant with spiky flowers and edible leaves, grows in all alpine-tundra regions throughout the Northern Hemisphere. This plant is also found on the arctic tundra. Voles and shrews are also common in all regions of alpine and arctic tundra.

It is important to note, however, that each of the world's major mountain systems also supports plants or animals that are unique to its alpine tundra. For example, the tiny, white snow buttercup is a flower found only on the tundra of the Rocky Mountains, where it blooms beneath the snow cover, gathering up moisture as the snow slowly melts. Muir's primrose was named after 19th-century American naturalist John Muir, who found these beautiful flowers sprouting in pink profusion at the edge of boulder fields only in the Sierra Nevada of California. The piper's harebell grows only in the cracks in rocks on the sides of the steep Olympic Mountains, on the coast of Washington. Chinchillas are small rodents with very soft gray coats. Valued for their fur, chinchillas were trapped almost to extinction. They are native only to the Andes Mountains, especially the high alpine tundra. They are very rare in the wild today.

Biologically speaking, mountaintops are like islands in the ocean. Species of plants and animals can be isolated from other, similar species for thousands of years. During that span of time, they may become so well adapted to the particular conditions on their mountains that they cannot survive anywhere else in the world. That is one way new kinds of plants and animals evolve. In a sense, mountaintops are one of nature's laboratories for developing new species. The rare, beautiful plants and agile, secretive animals that live only on our world's highest peaks are wonderfully adapted to one of the harshest environments on Earth.

A rare piper's harebell grows among colorful lichens in the Olympic Mountains in Washington State.

5

Threats to the Tundra

Rays of sunshine warm your shoulders, and a playful wind tousles your hair as you look across the arctic tundra. You are walking down a path that the caribou herds have tramped in their migrations to and from this summer-lush land. The wide sky is dotted with small, fluffy clouds. As you hike on the open tundra, you have the feeling that you are all alone in the world, wandering through a paradise untouched by the problems that plague other, more populated places.

But is it? There on the horizon is a faint but distinct line of yellow-gray haze. Air pollution. Near a large boulder, a steel animal trap shines silver in the sunlight. From a rise, you see a huge oil pipeline in the distance, snaking south for hundreds of miles. Then you hear a noise overhead that gets louder and louder until it is deafening. You cover your ears as an airplane zooms by. The tundra, like the other biomes, has suffered damage at the hands of human beings.

Opposite: Tunneling piles—destruction caused by mining for gold—wind through the tundra in the Yukon.

Threats to Tundra Animals: Past and Present

Tundra animals were overhunted more in the past than they are today. Musk oxen, for example, were wiped out on the Alaskan tundra and along the northeastern coast of Greenland in the late 1800s. Inuit and Indian hunters killed them and sold the meat to sailors on whaling ships, who were eager for fresh food. Musk oxen skins were also valued trade items. In the early 1900s, whole herds of musk oxen were decimated as animal collectors tried to capture young calves for zoos. The adult musk oxen would stand guard, completely encircling the young. The only way hunters could get to the calves was to slaughter the adults. By 1917, when Canada finally enacted laws to protect the musk oxen, only 500 of them survived on the tundra of Canada's mainland, with several thousand more living on isolated arctic islands. The musk oxen have recovered. Today, herds numbering about 40,000 thrive in Canada. The animals have been reintroduced to Alaska, where a herd of about 1,000 now lives.

Caribou, too, were subject to overhunting in the late 1800s and early 1900s. By 1950, the herds throughout North America were reduced by 90 percent. The caribou population has been recovering for the past fifty years, but many herds still have not reached their former numbers.

Today, many countries cooperate in setting limits, or quotas, on hunting musk oxen, caribou, arctic foxes, polar bears, and other animals of the arctic tundra. Protecting the tundra habitat, by setting up national parks and wildlife reserves, also helps protect tundra animals. For example, much of the Alaskan arctic tundra has been designated, for now, a wildlife refuge. An adjoining refuge in Canada gives the animals added protection.

Setting aside even a large area as a refuge does not mean that the animals that live there are completely safe. Pollutants released thousands of miles south of the arctic tundra have been showing up in tundra food chains. Animals take in toxic

pollutants, such as pesticides, when they feed. For example, a goose that winters in the southern United States may feed on plants that contain pesticides. The pesticides are stored in the goose's body. The goose then flies north to the arctic tundra, where it spends the summer. An arctic fox kills the goose and feeds it to its pups. Then a peregrine falcon kills and eats one of the fox pups. The pesticides are passed along each link in the food chain. The pollutants become more and more concentrated in animals near the top of the food chain, because the pesticides are stored in each animal's body and passed along to the next animal up the food chain. It is as if each animal on the food chain is eating all of the pesticides taken in by all of the animals below it on the food chain, plus the pesticides it eats directly itself.

A native Canadian hunts on the tundra, using a white screen for camouflage. Hunters must abide by government quotas set on hunting certain wildlife species.

51

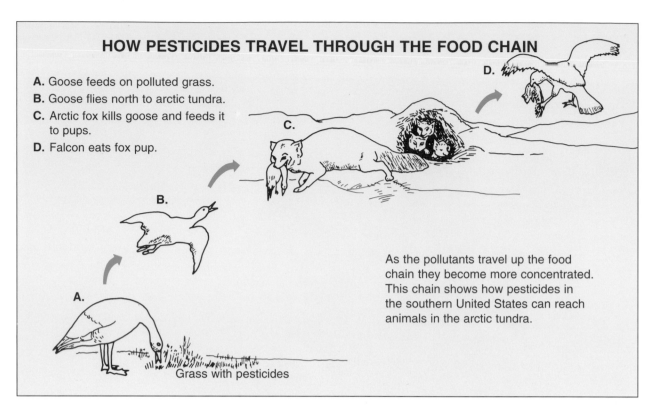

HOW PESTICIDES TRAVEL THROUGH THE FOOD CHAIN

A. Goose feeds on polluted grass.
B. Goose flies north to arctic tundra.
C. Arctic fox kills goose and feeds it to pups.
D. Falcon eats fox pup.

As the pollutants travel up the food chain they become more concentrated. This chain shows how pesticides in the southern United States can reach animals in the arctic tundra.

Grass with pesticides

Indirectly, pesticides have caused the deaths of thousands of young peregrine falcons. The pesticides weaken the birds' shells, and the eggs crack before the hatchlings are mature enough to survive. Because of this type of pollution, peregrine falcons have become an endangered species. Polar bears are also at risk for poisoning because of the buildup of pesticides and other pollutants in their bodies.

Mining and Oil Drilling

Some regions of the tundra are very rich in mineral resources. On the arctic tundra of Russia, coal, iron, nickel, aluminum, tin, tungsten, and gold are mined. Lead and zinc mines are found both on the arctic islands of Canada and on Greenland. Gold is mined on the arctic tundra of the Canadian mainland. Mineral exploration continues in many tundra areas. However, drilling for oil and natural gas is among the biggest and most controversial of the mining activities that take place on the arctic tundra. Alaska has a huge oil field at Prudhoe Bay. Canada maintains oil-drilling sites around the Mackenzie

Delta, where the river flows into the Beaufort Sea. Both the United States and Canada continue to search for more oil fields beneath the arctic tundra.

Mining and oil drilling threaten the tundra because they pollute the region's lakes and rivers, taint the air, and ravage the land. Harmful dust and gases are produced when mineral ores are separated from rocks during mining and when oil is pumped up from the ground during drilling. The gases and dust cause air pollution. When the dust settles on local lakes, ponds, rivers, and streams, the water becomes polluted. These air pollutants can also fall on the land, becoming concentrated in some areas and preventing plants from growing there. On some parts of the Russian tundra, the ground around nickel mines has become so contaminated that plants have died off completely and the soil has washed away.

Oil-drilling rigs, such as this one in Prudhoe Bay, Alaska, pollute the environment and threaten the wildlife of the tundra.

Mining and oil drilling scar the land. Bulldozers scoop out huge, open pits to uncover deposits of coal and iron. Oil derricks hundreds of feet tall punch out deep wells to tap underground oil fields. Tundra plants cannot grow in areas around mines and oil fields. Animals stay away from the noise and commotion of mining activities. If more mines are opened or oil drilling is expanded on the arctic tundra, the animals of the region may suffer greatly. Caribou and musk oxen feeding grounds, favored denning sites for polar bears, and essential

RUSSIA'S REINDEER-HERDING NENETS

Caribou roam the arctic tundra of North America and Greenland. Their close cousins, the reindeer, live on the arctic tundra of Europe and Asia. Caribou are generally wild. Reindeer, however, have been herded as semi-domestic animals for more than a thousand years. One group of people that still herd reindeer today are the Nenets of Russia's Yamal Peninsula.

In Nenet culture, about a dozen families work together to manage a herd of 5,000 reindeer. Every year, the group moves with the reindeer from their winter feeding grounds in the pine and spruce forest, to their summer pastures on the arctic tundra. The spring migration begins in March, when a thick blanket of snow still covers the forest and the rivers are still frozen solid. The trip, which covers more than 600 miles (965 kilo-meters), takes about three months. The Nenets travel by sleds, which are pulled by some of the reindeer. They sleep in cone-shaped tents made of reindeer skins, and they eat reindeer stew.

But Nenets who want to continue their traditional reindeer-herding lifestyle have been running into major obstacles. The Russian government, aided by American oil companies, has begun drilling for natural gas very close to the reindeer's summer pastures. Although it is against the law, people working for the gas company sometimes spend their leisure time hunting the reindeer. The gas company's guard dogs sometimes attack the reindeer. Even worse, huge tracts of grazing land have been lost to the gas wells. The fragile tundra vegetation has been destroyed by heavy machinery, and oil spills have spoiled once-pure lakes.

Some Nenets are hopeful that they can continue their traditional life-style despite the development of a huge gas field, now under construction, near the reindeer pastures. Others fear that the gas wells will spell the end of life as they know it, and they will herd reindeer no more.

Mining opera-
tions destroy
surrounding
land and drive
away animal life.
This abandoned
mine in St.
Elias, Alaska,
still litters the
tundra with
debris, even
though work has
stopped.

nesting grounds for migrating waterfowl may all be destroyed
if mining is increased on the tundra.

It is difficult to transport oil and minerals across the arctic tundra. There are few railroads, and not many roads are
open to large trucks. The sea freezes over for months, making
large-scale shipping impractical for at least half of the year.
One way to solve the problem of transporting one mineral—
oil—is with a pipeline. An oil pipeline thousands of miles long
has been built across Alaska. It carries oil from Prudhoe Bay,
on the north coast of the state, to Valdez, on the southern

coast. The port of Valdez remains open for year-round shipping. The pipeline runs across the route that the caribou traditionally take to and from their summer calving and feeding grounds. In places, the pipeline is raised many feet above the ground, so that the caribou can pass under it. The caribou do not seem to be bothered by the pipeline, but they do sometimes change course to avoid traffic on the road that runs beside the pipeline.

The biggest threat mining brings to the tundra is that of an oil spill, either on land or in the ocean. Oil spills destroy plants and kill animals. They pollute the ground and the water and can prevent life from returning to an area for decades or longer. A large oil spill either on the arctic tundra or in the ocean off the coast of the tundra could destroy huge regions of this fragile biome.

Barren ground caribou bulls pass under the Alaskan pipeline that runs right through their feeding and calving grounds.

Difficulties of Development

Building roads, towns, and airports is sometimes called developing a region. Development causes great difficulties on the tundra. Building techniques that work in other places do not work on the tundra. To remain stable, buildings and roads must have deep foundations. On the tundra, these foundations reach the permafrost. And because heat and pressure from the structure above can melt the permafrost, buildings sag and roads buckle. To build structures that will last on the tundra requires special techniques. For example, foundations can be refrigerated to keep them cold and to prevent them from thawing the permafrost.

Piping is also a problem on the tundra. In all other regions, pipes for water, fuel, and sewage can run underground, and usually there is little risk of the pipes' freezing. But pipes dug into the tundra would freeze because of contact with the permafrost. The pipes must be insulated or run aboveground in heated corridors. Such construction is costly to build and expensive to maintain.

Getting rid of waste causes still more problems for towns on the tundra. Because of the cold weather, sewage will not break down on the tundra. Garbage, too, cannot be effectively buried in the frozen land. Therefore, sewage and garbage must be shipped or piped to warmer regions. Again, this is costly, especially for large towns and cities.

Finally, tundra plants are very fragile. Most take years to recover from being stepped on even once. The trampling that occurs in an area when a building is erected, a road is cut, or an airstrip is paved wipes out most plants in that area for many, many years. Without plant cover, the tundra's thin soil washes away. The region becomes barren and incapable of supporting life.

The arctic tundra is a vast region. No matter how rich its resources, however, the arctic tundra cannot support huge populations of people. Overdevelopment of the tundra will not

WINTER ROADS ACROSS THE TUNDRA

Roads in the arctic tundra are so rare that, at least in the winter, many people cut across the tundra, not on pavement, but on ice. Lakes form natural highways in the winter: When the ice that covers the lakes is about 3 feet (1 meter) thick, a snowplow clears a path, and cars and trucks have a smooth road for hundreds of miles.

However, problems exist with these winter roads. Winds can whip up the snow, making it impossible to follow the plowed path. Blizzards can dump several feet of snow and leave motorists stranded on the ice for days. Without several days' extra supply of fuel, people traveling on these roads could easily freeze to death. The roads are sometimes impassable even after a heavy snowfall has been cleared. The weight of the snow can press down on the ice, causing water to seep up through small cracks in the ice. No vehicle can be driven on a surface as slippery as water-covered ice.

The worst potential problem, however, is an obvious one. If the weather warms up and the ice gets too thin, a car or truck could fall through the ice and sink to the bottom of the lake. This could be disastrous, not only for the passengers, but for the entire tundra region. Many of the vehicles that travel these ice-plowed roads carry toxic substances to and from mining communities and other towns. If a truck carrying diesel fuel, for instance, sank in an inland lake, it would eventually break apart, releasing the fuel into the lake. This would pollute the lake and any other bodies of water that the lake flows into. These other bodies of water could carry the fuel all the way to the ocean, damaging all plant and animal life in its path. One sunken truck could mean the deaths of thousands upon thousands of tundra organisms.

only destroy this biome but will wreak havoc with all living things on Earth. Large-scale destruction of the permafrost would change the drainage patterns of rivers and deprive many southern regions of their water supply. Air pollution in the tundra could cause the climate to heat up. A warmer climate would cause the ice in the Arctic Ocean to melt. Ocean levels would rise, and the world's coastal cities would flood. A change in the climate of the Arctic would also change weather patterns throughout the world, causing floods or droughts in the world's prime farmlands. With the destruction of the tundra, all living things would have to adjust to drastic changes. Or they might even perish.

It is very unlikely that the tundra will suffer the complete destruction described here. People throughout the world have begun to value the tundra, not only for its resources, but for the power it holds as a symbol of the hardiness of life and the adaptability of nature. The tundra is our world's last remote, unspoiled land region. As such, it presents a pristine vastness, a breathing space in which to contemplate humankind's deepest potential. All of the other biomes have been altered to a great degree by our activities, by our desire to bend nature to our needs. The tundra remains, reminding us that nature has its own terms. If we appreciate those terms, we will preserve the tundra for future generations, who may look to it for inspiration in restoring and preserving all the biomes of our planet.

A polar bear mother and her cub wander across the serene beauty of the arctic tundra—one of our world's natural treasures.

59

Glossary

adaptation A characteristic of an organism that makes it suited to live or reproduce in a particular environment.

alpine Referring to mountains. The alpine tundra is the biome found at the top of high mountains that includes miniature trees and other low-lying plants.

arctic Referring to the northernmost part of the earth.

biome A community of specific types of plants, animals, and other organisms that covers a large area of the earth.

camouflage To blend in with the surroundings, especially by matching the color or shapes of the background.

evaporate The process of water turning into a gas.

food chain The order in which different organisms feed on one another in a given community.

food web A diagram that shows the feeding relationships among different organisms in a community.

glacier A thick sheet of ice that covers an area of land. Glaciers form on high mountains and on the earth's polar regions.

hibernation A state of very deep sleep in which body temperature and heart rate drop very low. Some tundra animals hibernate during the winter to help them survive the cold.

insulate To hold at a steady temperature. On the tundra, animals and plants have adaptations to help hold in heat.

krummholz A forest of willows, birches, and evergreen trees, all under a few feet tall, that grows on the tundra.

larva The immature form of an insect that has not yet metamorphosed, or changed, to its adult form.

lichen An association of algae and fungi living together as a single unit.

mammal A warm-blooded animal that has body hair, gives birth to live young, and produces milk to feed to its young.

migrate To move seasonally or periodically, from one region or climate to another.

Northern Hemisphere The northern half of the earth.

organism Any living thing, such as a plant, animal, fungus, or bacterium.

permafrost A layer of permanently frozen ground that lies beneath the tundra surface. It also exists in patches in certain other biomes.

pesticides Chemicals that farmers and others use to kill insects and pests that threaten plants.

photosynthesis The process by which plants use the energy from sunlight to make sugars, which they use for food.

pingo A circular or oval hill that forms on the tundra because of a blister of ice pushing up on the land.

pollutants Harmful chemicals or materials that are released into the air, water, or onto the land.

predator An animal that hunts other animals for food.

prey An animal that is hunted by another animal.

reproduction The process by which an organism creates new individuals of the same species.

Southern Hemisphere The southern half of the earth.

species A group of animals or plants whose members can interbreed and produce fertile offspring.

summer solstice The longest day of the year. In the Northern Hemisphere, the summer solstice falls on June 21; in the Southern Hemisphere, the summer solstice falls on December 21.

winter solstice The shortest day of the year. In the Northern Hemisphere, the winter solstice falls on December 21; in the Southern Hemisphere, the winter solstice falls on June 21.

For Further Reading

Alexander, Bryan, and Alexander, Cherry. *Inuit.* Madison, New Jersey: Raintree Steck-Vaughn Publishers, 1992.

Barrett, N.S. *Polar Animals.* New York: Franklin Watts, 1988.

Ekoomiak, Normes. *Arctic Memories.* New York: Henry Holt and Company, 1990.

Hiscock, Bruce. *Tundra: The Arctic Land.* New York: Atheneum, 1986.

James, Barbara. *Conserving the Polar Regions.* Madison, New Jersey: Raintree Steck-Vaughn Publishers, 1990.

Kalman, Bobbie, and Belsey, William. *An Arctic Community.* New York: Crabtree Publishing Company, 1988.

Lambert, David. *Our World: Polar Regions.* Morristown, New Jersey: Silver Burdett Press, 1987.

Reynolds, J. *Far North: Vanishing Cultures.* San Diego: Harcourt Brace and Company, 1992.

Index

Acknowledgments and Photo Credits

Cover and page 13: ©Stephen J. Krasemann/Photo Researchers, Inc.; pp. 6, 15: ©Kim Heacox/Peter Arnold, Inc.; pp. 10, 11, 22: ©Fred Bruemmer/Peter Arnold, Inc.; p. 14: ©Mark Stouffer/Earth Scenes; pp. 16, 19: ©Johnny Johnson/Animals Animals; p. 20: ©Lowell Georgia/Photo Researchers, Inc.; p. 21: ©Bob Armstrong/Animals Animals; p. 24: ©Joe McDonald/Earth Scenes; p. 26: ©M & C Photography/Peter Arnold, Inc.; p. 28: ©Thomas D. Mangelsen/Peter Arnold, Inc.; p. 30: ©Jeff Lepore/Photo Researchers, Inc.; p. 34: ©Georges Dif/Peter Arnold, Inc.; p. 35 (top): ©Marty Cooper/Peter Arnold, Inc.; p. 35 (bottom): ©Jim Zipp/Photo Researchers, Inc.; p. 36: ©Norbert Rosing/Oxford Scientific Films/Earth Scenes; p. 39: ©Chlaus Lotscher/Peter Arnold, Inc.; pp. 40, 46: ©Ray Richardson/Animals Animals; p. 44: ©Alan Carey/Photo Researchers, Inc.; p. 47: ©Richard Kolar/Earth Scenes; p. 48: ©Brian Milne/Earth Scenes; p. 51: ©Brian Milne/Earth Scenes; p. 53: ©Randy Brandon/Peter Arnold, Inc.; p. 55: ©Rich Reid/Earth Scenes; p. 56: ©Leonard Lee Rue III/Animals Animals; p. 59: ©Dan Guravich/Photo Researchers, Inc.
Artwork and graphics by Blackbirch Graphics, Inc.